# We Help Our Community

What's the Pro[...]

I0901522

Sadie Silva

COMPUTER SCIENCE For the REAL World™

Rosen Classroom™

Our class wants to give back to our community. What can we do to help out?

First, my teacher asks us a question. "What's one problem that needs to be solved in our community?"

Our community center helps children in need. Sometimes the children need books to read.

We will collect books for them! First, we need to tell people about our book drive.

Some students make signs.
They hang the signs in
our school.

Some students send e-mails to teachers. The e-mails tell teachers about the book drive.

Some students write letters about the book drive. Each student takes a letter home.

My class sets up tables in front of our school. It's time to gather books!

People bring books about science and history. They bring books with stories, too.

We drop the books off at our community center. Our book drive was a success!

# Words to Know

community center

e-mail

sign